The Truth about A

In his interpretation of Antigone, Seamus Heaney says, 'Nobody can be sure they are always right.' Maureen O'Shaughnessy's *The Truth about A* further attends to this idea through various readings of the myth as portrayed by Sophocles, Brecht, Ted Hughes, Anne Carson and, most particularly, Euripides. Set in contemporary Sydney, among a fictional underworld family, *The Truth about A* not only considers the issue of whether to obey the law or your conscience but delves into the nature of the creative impulse and the eternal bonds and chasms between generations. Antigone, daughter of Oedipus and Jocasta, provokes the fury of the crime overlord Creon with her profound sense of honour, family and duty. But this spirit of defiance raises questions infinitely more complex than the brute facts of power and order, engendering a meditation on justice, ethics and personal judgement.

For M.A.

Maureen O'Shaughnessy

The Truth about A

Also by Maureen O'Shaughnessy and published by Ginninderra Press
Lakeland

The Truth about A
ISBN 978 1 76041 359 0
Copyright © Maureen O'Shaughnessy 2017

First published 2017 by
GINNINDERRA PRESS
PO Box 3461 Port Adelaide 5015 Australia
www.ginninderrapress.com.au

Myth is a story that can be retold by anyone, with infinite variation, and still be recognisable as itself.

– James Meek

I go back to the scene of the crime
hard, bright places,
so much so that when I wake up it seems a lie that I should still be alive…

– Roberto Bolaño

her coordinates

    Antigone sat up in bed like bush in the breeze,
(passing over her shoulders sun fingered the TV, black
in silver brackets on the marble wall.)

Has she time to execute the mild loosening of yoga?
Her analyst has filled her ears with the necessity
    of attentions to the body, especially
given the road she wants to take and the

    difficulties of performing.

Antigone sings a long slow note, keeping her pitch through the low places
and smoothing the distance around her limbs.

    Her mother's name is Jocasta.
She wants Antigone to practise hard, go on TV and sing on X-factor.

    Antigone thinks she would rather die.

    So many things
her mother doesn't understand about what hurts inside her.

    Her mother is the family troubleshooter. She's a faded beauty.
    When Antigone was born and arranged in her arms
she said, *You know, small flowers leave just as much pollen up your nose.*

    Antigone began barricading herself against the world early on.

    There was orange juice and her phone
on a table beside her by the wide rumpled bed, and she thought,

> I'm totally worn out by the night's dreaming.
> I wake up and the morning carries the lost voices,
> the lost faces I'll never see again,
> and I don't know what
> on earth they're trying to tell me.

'Don't fret,' her analyst likes to say. 'The darkness of our dreams is a souvenir to inspire us.'

Yet a different thought extends from Antigone's mind; it's more like when the mental bank opens its administrative branch.

In daylight, her eyes become very deep cavities in an over-lit room.

her father

When Antigone was a child her father, Oedipus, taking her into town, always just her (usually just her), would drive the Mercedes with the top down. The car howled through the rock bluffs of Oyster Bay to the King Street office.

There was an undercover car park.
Pigeons roosted and cooed like drains,
or like drowning geese. Antigone and her father
walked up the two flights of stairs under
the fluorescent lights and in the echoing drear
to where his room was, sun falling
through a tall window from the west.

A whole childhood gliding by under flaring sunlight.

Looking down to York Street in the summer afternoons the year that her brother Polyneices left, Antigone would find herself thinking of the apocalypse –

huge new stores, huge crowds,
people moving across the world,
eyes lowered and without much sense of delight,
in a kind of commercial procession…

Back then, Barack Obama and Kevin Rudd dominated
public spirit and the word 'apology'
could be hidden under the tongue,
its sound
more a colour than a word.

Summer evenings in some cities were filled with smoke:
then it was a disease thing, a virus sprung from pigs:
   then she'd heard about more dropped children in the sea
and the country with its unappeasable people
   turned in on itself.
It was a time of wishing that
there were ways to get things right.

Antigone didn't know who she was,
didn't think she really fitted in with anyone. She loved her mother
and her sister and two brothers, but most of all

   she loved her dad.

'My princess,' is what he would
call her, even while her sister's eyes
would drop with shy fresh pain behind a heavy black fringe
whenever she heard this.
She'd smile, but you could tell ultimately she was pained at Antigone
constantly using things to her own benefit.
Ismene stayed at home.

In the car, head on his shoulder, Antigone would say,
   'Can we go shopping?' in a voice
that wanted to make a good impression,
   because a girl shopping with her Papa felt like a glimpse of desire,
   a glimpse of pretending at grown-up power.

In this way they cruised the city's centre each Saturday:
department stores, arcades and boutiques and –
always in the middle of the day, especially if it was hot –

milkshakes in the café: old parlour wood,
the glass-fronted cabinet full of iced cupcakes,
the spiky green pot plants; her father, smiling,
forgetting to hide his teeth, chipped, one missing,
her chest twitching so much inside from some sort of blend
    of fear and joy
    she couldn't speak;
tea smells, frilled collars, sometimes the crumbs
made constellations, spread across the polished oak of the table,
often they got stuck under her nails;
the resident waitress, 'Hello love, how're you, the usual? –'
she's short, in her fifties, the sickly sweet scent of lavender and cotton
wafting from her arms, rolling out serviettes and cutlery,
'Malted vanilla, strawberry, straws in the container over there, why not
spoil yourselves – I daresay you've plenty more places to get to,'
    and Antigone would shrug, not really interested.
She just kept her eyes on her father, who was
    a king, a poet, a spokesman.
It was difficult to describe, as now,
the sense she had that her name
was like some nonentity's read in a women's magazine,
and that the man sitting before her with
the gold chain around his neck was the head
of a company whose rank in business
was well known everywhere from his financial
support for causes to do with cancer and heart research,
and the think tank he started for the nation in matters of foreign affairs,
and the special privileges he had provided
for members of his family, and

also because his wife,
she seemed out of place; she was older…

    Yes, yes,
    this man, Oedipus,
who always had the last word, without opposition –
    Antigone saw
that he was thinking of her, but then others.

    Yes,

    yes,

he was the strongest man in those days, still in command.
    He filled her with a hankering, and pride.

    But that was long ago.

swollen foot

He knew a rival once, for Jocasta's flaming eye,
a man called Laius. He was the great public figure
with hair like rope under an iron helmet
who didn't care what he banged, the perfect assassin.
The word was he had a habit of murders,
his shoulders were the width of the rafters,
riding his chopper mile after mile,
teaching the younger men how to drive,
how to drive fast and to drive with faultless cop-avoiding skills
    through the city's underworld.

Oedipus thought this was a shifty old man,
(who it was rumoured had once kidnapped the son of his host,
taking the open-mouthed boy as a fox would a kid:
he had acted in bad faith). When Oedipus met him on
the road, under the tinselling winds of autumn,
Laius patronised him. Oedipus was in the act
of confronting him, trying to snatch back facts from the years gone,
but instead felt the swivelling of wheels on one foot.
So he killed Laius with two blows, and all
    but one of his gang.

oedipus speaks

Thursday nights at the trots.

The track. The city
as its backdrop. And where I'd meet certain members.
And where we did business, watching the dark brown
push of the horses pinned to their sulkies out
the corners of our eyes, and draw,
now and then – thin, brassy, uplifting slackness and
a hundred times kinder than wives –
the mistresses.

Imagine my life is what it once was; the firm,
the bedroom, the yacht, the racecourse.
The inner suburbs a good area in which to control things
and I held the reins.

And everyone I knew
did what I told them, whether it was to get
what they wanted, or keep their jobs.

Then,
Tiresias' text, 7.55 p.m. Spring Carnival, 2015,
lines like scratch marks on glass

> Just the two of us. Meet me at the bar in ten.
> You'll have to accept my apologies in advance
> for being the bearer, as they say.
> Prepare for a shock. You'll wish your eyes saw as
> little as mine.

What's this about?

> You'll see.

> Give me 20. I want to lay 5K on Europa Star.
>> Maybe pick up beers. Words not good, I'm afraid.

So it was. The sin in my marriage revealed.

My wife,
    Jocasta,
not quite as she appeared.

    Today I know the flesh of my autobiography is inside her.
    I remember the shock of it.

    'Cursed!' we said. 'Our creation in each other
and in each other creating our relation.'

    Our enemies observing the growing dissent and calamity with delight,
'You know how pride comes before a fall.'

    We felt a backhanded show of support at the company.

    A rush of cool wind across our territory.

And then, spreading strife,
the family enterprise turned wobbly where it had thrived,
    our sons, at loggerheads and in a desperate state. And before long they strike –

    'Goddamn moron! Dropkick!
Should Tiresias lend you a dress?'

    What they wanted was proud, infernal power.

And these are the moments when you realise that you've walked up
a blind alley, that you've a blind spot, you're blind as a bat,
it's become a case of the blind leading the blind, that men
are blind in their own cause, that you're flying blind
and you'll have to turn a blind eye; and
though everyone will try to swear blind it's otherwise
that a nod is as good as a wink to blind horse.

    Still, I lowered my head and let them fight.
    My sons –
I gave them a last broken look.
    I could see nothing of what I wanted,
tired and empty.

    My eyes have been drained out, yes,
and I can no longer see the days go –

    the tender pods, the pools of blue out the window –

things being worse, I imagine my daughters –
hit by such shame, my god. Like the palms here on the steep subsided shore
of Oyster Bay they grip, and sway to and fro,
    flinging their quarrels out into the open.

    I think perhaps I've learned something of the differences
between men and women.

    But then, of course, hindsight is always hindsight.

further along

At the moment the two brothers discovered
their father had made them from something deformed
they saw the wounds appearing;
 'There goes the future,' they said, 'if we don't take hold.'

So they went up to his study, grabbed Oedipus by the shoulders,
dragged him to the basement and propped him in the corner.
Above the window was the cctv: Polyneices took a chair across, drove
a billiard cue into the camera's lens and smashed it.
Knives of sun cut the dark.
Eteokles, smiling sweatily,
cracked his weapon on his father's cries. They were in charge now.

Dressed in a flashy suit, Eteokles
continued to blast commands into his father's face, his fat, damp hands
holding onto whatever hair still held to Oedipus's head.
Him, gob-smacked and shaken. Too resigned by this point
to even protest. Polyneices tries to calm his brother down,
 (*Fucking bastard, fucking bastard*, under his breath).

Oedipus thinks he's going to die.

After the clamour, the pieces of skin-hair and the floor sucking
up blood and disorder.
 Then Eteokles and Polyneices,

telling their mother that the usurping has been carried out.

.

specific questions

    Sky changes colour. Eteokles, Polyneices and their mother.
The three of them exposing themselves to what frightens
yet emboldens them
and arguing with it, examining it.
The two girls upstairs.
Eteokles speaks,
he's already got his business cards printed up.
The story is he will oversee things for one year and then,
the following year, Polyneices.
Eteokles and Polyneices hammer ideas at each other for hours,
but the resolutions keep slipping.
Eventually, Polyneices bows out.
He packs.
Goes.

daughters

Yes, those two talk about music,
and games, and festivals and TV shows and fitness,
and they're always trying to come up
with ways to make themselves heard,
never letting themselves get into a position
where they have to see, much less listen
to the man of little importance I have become.

Do I blame them?

Ah no, it's not something they should understand.

Sometimes, when I'm feeling my way in the dark
down passageways to find where meals are set,
I get excited by their voices.
I listen to the talk going forward and back –
I've noticed the women mostly speak
and their brother hugs long silences –
also I keep my ears open for singing:
Ismene plays guitar,
her sister tapping, singing
love songs… Hearing them playing together,
   I love that,
my heart tunnelling under the door and along the floor.

In this way Oedipus appeases his vacant sockets, gets through each day unable to take in light, but with hands straight out in front to guide him.

occupations

Antigone had lived with her family in the Palis compound for sixteen years; she was growing up now and couldn't decide what she wanted to do. She had tried for a job at the local McDonalds as a junior. She was given a role in the kitchen, made all the nuggets. Those fryers were hot, filled with boiling oil. The heat rose and caked grease onto any bit of exposed skin. One day, when they were short-staffed, she was given a shift at the front counter by her manager; he was thirty-one and ran the franchise like a forgotten veteran of some war. For Antigone, it was a welcome change to work on the registers, racking up numbers and chatting to customers with their appetites hooked in their throats. The registers had a measured efficiency, shiny and squat in their positions side by side. Whenever a customer came shuffling across the grey tiles with a fat wallet in hand, Antigone would ask how they were doing. Tap the order into coded keys and pictures would light up S SMALL M MEDIUM L LARGE. It was curious. The customers were people who laughed and frowned at the same time. At the service desk you could step up, you could step back, you could chew things over while you waited in the queue.

Later that day, Antigone had her big fallout. She was alone at the counter, serving a tense couple, the patience she'd had earlier now fine as a fly wing. She had keyed in the order, but they couldn't decide if they wanted to eat there or out. Antigone stood not looking at them but straight up at the TV. They were arguing between angry breaths and every few seconds one of them would put their hands on hips and turn a half circle of exasperation. Leaning across the counter, 'What the hell!' Antigone finally said. She was fired on the spot.

When she got home, her mother and brother were sitting in a quiet room. 'Why aren't I surprised? You never stick at anything,' said Jocasta, when she heard the news. There were pictures on the computer in front of her, bright faces done up to the hilt. She wore a sarong and white linen blouse; her throat was bare, her feet. On the arm of the sofa beside her was her empty glass, her necklace, her slip-ons.

Antigone flinched. The words fell on her, stinging. What hurt her more than ever was that she, as it happened, considered spoilt by hers siblings, had been the first to find work outside the family business when getting a job, whereas all of the others hadn't.

Dusk, yellow light in stripes on the floor, the windows wide open. She was thrown, she was crying. She was shaking with short, regular stresses, like the snipping of grasses, like a child. Her sobs were startling, her cheeks red. She was stammering shreds of sound, of rage, of blame. Her shirtsleeves, grubby, way below her wrists. Her mother didn't bat an eye.

Outside, the boats uncurl and tumble on the horizon until the sun stops.

are you happy, antigone?

'Are you happy, Antigone?' her analyst asks.
She smiles at him before she answers, a small, coquettish smile.

'I do my best. I don't know that happiness is so important, I really don't. Happiness is something you want in theory, not in practice. I'd like to make my mark, though. I want to make something good. What are my options? I have so many pains, so many sore spots.'

Your father…' he said.

'Yes.'

'He's very successful.'

'I know, but I don't believe in all that. I think it's quite escapist.'

'Escapist. I see, it could be, but the effects are very disturbing.'

'Why disturbing?'

'Well, he's clearly selfish,' he said.

'I hate that word.'

'It's appropriate.'

'No, it isn't.'

'I see, so what word would you choose?'

'One word?'

'Yes.'

'Letdown.'

'Letdown?'

'Yes. She folds her arms behind her head. 'He's a letdown. He made a mistake and gave me a terrible life.'

The analyst nods. She tells him about the songs she has written. It is just to give him an idea; he will understand her better.

'Well, Antigone,' he says, 'A little progress.'

She is a slender girl, clenched hands, a pair of a battered Converse on her feet, a slight curve in her shoulders and chest.

'What kind of things do you like to sing about?' he says.

'Love. Of course. The problem of finding it.'

He is writing in his notebook.

'I don't fit in with most people,' she explains.

'It's sometimes difficult to fit in.'

'And still – in my case,' she says, '*no one* is more unfair than my mother. To her I'm dangerous. Emma Bovary said it was her nerves that stopped her being happy as a mother, but what stops mine is that she's always absolutely sure that she's right and that I'm wrong. For as I long as I can remember that's what she's said.'

'Doesn't she encourage your music?

'Oh, she'd like it if I – as she calls it – *got somewhere with it*,' said Antigone. 'But then, when she sees me sing, wearing a short skirt and getting attention, her face grows rigid. Absolutely rigid.'

various sums

 In the Philippines there are plenty of business options.
 It takes enterprise,
but there is opportunity. There are hot days
when birds sail into the green-eyed trees
and moor there in the branches' crooks for hours,
 like tiny inflatable outboards in the coves
of Oyster Bay; but labour and commodities are cheap.

30 on the pay roll most loyal to Polyneices went with him to Manila.
20 to work on the venture, 5 as personal staff, 5 as bodyguards:
 companies usually start out small
yet can quickly build to a position of market domination.
 Within a month of arrival,
Polyneices was running a firm
that took up a whole block near the centre of town.

 In Manila he flexed his broad chest, his determination,
embedded in his business, measuring
 out the weeks of his practical migration until the time came
when he would return to Palis, take the helm.

palis

    A driveway cutting the guts of the garden
and massive steps at the end of it:

    sloping around the margins two Rottweilers
shedding drool from galvanised tongues
    and a metal grille between you and the manservant

    as the camera drones to angle its eye and you turn inwards, while,
twitching like a frightened pony,
you concentrate on it screwed in iron to the brickwork

    till tin-knuckled hands reach down and unlock
the padlocked door and let you in.

rights

    All in a rush Eteokles' hour to hand over had come.
A thousand protests in his heart –

he couldn't climb down his desire.

    Twenty kilometres away from him, Polyneices
took the hire car along the road that lay between the airport and the shire.

As everyone at Palis waited for his approach –

    an army of them,
the clang of gates knocking eastwards from the headland,
employees moving over the lawns like orb spiders –

Eteokles, a terrible sweep of determination igniting
    his bearded slatted mouth,
advanced with the hairy red bulges of resolve inside him to the entrance,
    a handgun in each pocket,
so that no one would show a flash of fear
or utter a word to jeopardise the operation.

    He planted his feet, thick and sturdily shod, on the path, facing
the secured access. He shielded his eyes. Squinted.

Armed guards bark to the ranks,
    'Positions everyone!'

    Eteokles thought of the moment when his brother
would pull up to the intercom, waves of insects darting towards him,
yellow pourings of sun shifting over his shoulders where the trees
    had been cut back to clear the field of vision.

And the wind started to paddle, then swim,
then wade over the walls in swell after swell of gusts,

    the blasts so jerky,
so erratic that the wire balls
distributed along the rim began to spin on themselves.

    But the car,

    long,

    black,

    slid into sight, not flinching, smooth as oil.

    Eteokles could see a row of chaperones behind Polyneices,
erecting patterns in the seat.

    I want what's mine again, thought Eteokles. *Now we're set.*

    As the tides.

    As the day.

    This is the house I dream of. No man will come between.

    He and his brother hanging tough.
Tethered as tandem sky-jumpers fall,
    still bound together
while hurtling to the ground.

pang

All summer the crack and thrash of ageing bones…

These days, Antigone never has anything to do with her father.

There's nothing but emptiness behind his eyelids.

Her analyst claims it's a
    conversion disorder,
what mental health professionals once called

    hysterical blindness.

Antigone hollers at her sister inside her room in full honed voice –

    'The shape of our lives has been moulded by tradition, patriarchy, capitalism! So little of our own form self-devised, it is unacceptable! It should not be accepted!'

the bronze bolts

    To the rooftop, where the smell
of things sprouting eats up
the cloud-patched air.
Jocasta tows Antigone
up the stairs
leading to the door.
It is a painted metal hatch
containing many bolts,
the surface scuffy, flaked.
(Antigone would have preferred
to keep watch below,
from her room.
But her analyst had advised, 'Go,
see with your mother
your brother
arriving home.')
Jocasta punches in code,
walks quickly out; Antigone
follows, uneasily.
She peers over the ledge:
limestone ridges veering east
over houses, trees, streets.
The cove running backwards
from a steady stream of sludge.
She sees the car flashing
around the bend. And Polyneices
with his wife,
in the back seat, all lord
and master; five attendants in dark glasses
sitting with him: a whole army

of square-shouldered agents
driving in the rear.
Beyond the Palis walls,
Eteokles' hired hands
still stake their marked positions.
The sight of which makes Antigone shriek
and her mother's nipples
stand on end.
Oh what a noise there is,
carrying loud and long and sharp.
Jocasta feels the cut of it
right down in her ears.
When she finally looks
over at Antigone it is with a mix
of pride and fear:
she says, 'You are your father's daughter, clearly,
but guard against
such open alleys of feeling –
excess is an end to everything
when the heroics totter over.'

outside

    It is late afternoon.

Polyneices at the gate.

Barging through.

'Brother and back-stabbing dog!'

Shots all round.

The way the toadies pull their weapons.

The way Jocasta races down the stairs.

'Antigone! Come with me! Will this heartbreak never end?'

Raises her arms reflexively in front of her face.

Eteokles swivels his feet in the gravel.

'Mother, I won't allow what I've worked for to be taken from me!'

And takes aim as Polyneices whips his piece from his belt
to blow off Eteokles' head, and collapses in the crossfire.

the life of death

    Poor ambitious Eteokles is killed

    and Polyneices too, packed with cartridges,
packed with flies, spread like sleepers on the drive.

    The sun hit the drying blood in shafts
as soft as salmon in a pool. Shocked attendants.
They dragged them by the legs to shady ground,
took off their jackets, covered the bodies.

    They tried to put the lids to sleep
but the brothers' eyes kept yawning.
Between the canopy and moss. What leaked into the earth
    sank as a black ooze.

    Eteokles' henchman grabbed Polyneices' wife,
threatened to hang her from the gantry.
    He beat her, smeared his blood-stained hand
across her breast, threw her to her knees.

    Coming apart like thunder, the sound was astounding:
madness, the clamour of the inconsolable.
Poor ambitious Eteokles killed, and Polyneices, too.

torment

When the police arrived, bulled by roaring engines, Jocasta bored into her palms, weeping with homicidal grief, struggling to breathe.

Then her chest twitched and she lifted her face, a veteran fighter.

eyewitness

We were on the footpath across the road and the bay was sparkly grey. A line of dark-coloured cars crawled along the shore and smoke from a cigarette came out the window of the one in front. Bad eggs, nothing but trouble, said my eldest boy, pulling his cap over his brows. The fact is there are all sorts of crooks living in that house with their cameras and their dogs. Ten metres from where I am right now, the limo pulled up. I got my phone out of my trouser pocket and stepped back behind the telegraph pole. Saw close up one of the sons getting out. He's big, with blond hair and fat lips. He looks around, goes up to the intercom, jiggles his neck: walls high as the house, trees, in a street that used to be for young families. He leans in toward the speaker in a cream suit and hat. With his thumb he presses the buzzer to be let in. No one answers, he pulls out a firearm, flicks the chamber, and shoots at the gate. Just one time. A guard, hidden behind an urn, watches the lock buckle. He's massive and they raise their guns at each other. They don't say anything but suddenly the place is swarming. Can't tell how, but some way they must have signalled to their respective sides, like game on, take aim, there's a showdown on the cards, ready, and watch your backs. On the porch it's hysterics. The mother waving and shrieking, with the family's daughters and the family's dogs. Small white flashes of shooting. Twisted and rigid, the shot-at guys look like Hollywood extras. The cops turn up. Tell us everything you saw. Big guys, I say. Like a gang? The bunch are well known to the force but they feign ignorance. The mob that live there are high fliers but they've also been on the law's wrong side. Up the drive, I see the woman, still snooty but she's broken-hearted. Her head is buried under the hair tumbling down one of her girls' necks. The detectives swoop in: bullshit faces that say you'll be okay when really you're not okay. The other daughter watches the scene for a long time, arms wrapped round herself, then is led inside. End of the show.

Amazing to think what goes on under our very noses, isn't it? Certain images keep re-playing over in my mind now: the dark cars and the glittery bay, the gate with the dog snarling behind it, the guard and the stone urn, the daughter who held herself apart. There's no reason why it's one fragment and not another that presses in on my memory. A pale shadow passes on the other side of an upper storey window. The girl pacing the floor of her room in despair? Who's to know. All these reporters asking questions, how many men, what sort of guns, what did we see. If we turn on the Channel 9 news tonight, will we see us? Tonight on the TV, is it us that we'll see?

relationship

The analyst takes her call, extends his learning on Antigone's words, 'What fury! What despair!' she cries. 'I was speechless for a moment and then I asked them whether they thought my brothers had actually managed to aim their guns and shoot each other at exactly the same time, because I reckon things like that only happen on CSI.'

'Yes,' said her analyst, 'I know what you mean, but it's possible it's true. The thing is, at this point it isn't like the minute of their deaths directs reality or what's awaiting you, a very good reason to consider how far you should go. And to what depths.'

at the morgue

    Seven men in rows on metal slabs,
the fluids leaking out, the formaldehyde flowing in,
in the galleys of the room.
    They took a bullet for the cause.

    There was a man, the new boss,
Creon, Jocasta's brother.
It came to him to identify
the fresh killed bodies.

    As it happened, he and
his son, Haemon,
had long-held fantasies
that involved Antigone – an idea

had risen between them –
one day the two
might be a couple: now
would they be together?

    A sea of disturbed sensation
washes through Creon's limbs,
    a great wave of rage
at Polyneices' headstrong charge.

    A memory runs in; the 3 a.m. call:
    'Give aid, give backup in the fight.
You've got to see that I, Eteokles,
am better suited than my brother to this job.

What has Polyneices done for us?
I know how to run my father's firm,
the one others have faith in;
I am favoured to survive.

See, if you look closely into the world
where my brother has his interests
you'll find everything hinging
on wheels of greed, while here

the mob is fused,
a great tower of business
established over time,
mortared stone by stone.

Think of his staff,
all those braggers and women,
not from here,
but from there,

a place of scattered islands
buffeted by winds,
a pocked irregular terrain
half swallowed by the ocean;

his wife, alongside him, urging
    "Gather quick, pack quick
    fellow agents,
    we've got to fly south in force

to where the white parrots squawk like mad
and sharks swim with open mouths,
on the trail of my husband's brother,
who is cheating him of his place.

Take your best official jackets
and tuck neat pieces in your pants
or go out and select the kind of knife
no officer will seize from you,

then hire cars and steer them through
the tunnels when the traffic's light,
at late afternoon, when the sun
glides across the skin of the rooves,

and drive out to Oyster Bay
where you'll mobilise and carve a path
to the doors of Palis, bulwark
of the corrupt family seat."

This is what I discovered in the email
that my mole passed on to me –
small shrill sounds of envy
manifested in Polyneices through his wife.
So she wrapped her will and skin
to effect, draping
her sordid plans
like a sheet around him.'

Now, a blood star on Eteokles' forehead,
a crater in Polyneices' chest,

as each lies flat on a silver table
under a blank clock's stare.

palis that afternoon

'It is against you and everyone that Polyneices stood over us,' Jocasta told her daughters, 'and *WE WILL NOT BURY HIM.*'

'Mother,' said Antigone, 'don't you know? It's in the name of love not absolution that a funeral is held!'

'I know you mean well,' said Jocasta, 'but that's how it is! I won't talk any more about it!'

the dogs turn

Ismene and Antigone had lived in Palis for more than seventeen years, and not a year went by when they didn't get a new pet of some kind. They had no preference for any particular species. They had accumulated a range of different animals, many of whom met each other in the house or garden with the uneasy suspicion that things could get troublesome here, because here, in that massive fortressed compound, is where they just might run out of room.

Antigone especially gave herself over to the animals and whatever they required; the dogs, the cats, her brothers' snakes in the aquarium, the birds in the aviary. Each animal spoke to her, imprisoned in fortune's making, as if to stir her confidence. Dressed in the peachy cloth of professional dancers, hair in a knob on her head, she was trailed by the Rottweilers and white poodles. The cats would stiffen, the flocks of finches would cry out as she passed, Here! Here!

Haemon dropped by, and, still fighting back tears, she took him to see the serpents. Each aquarium had a wooden cover and a lamp on top as part of the thermal gradient needed: the snakes tended to stay curled behind the rocks piled in the corner. On that afternoon, Antigone and Haemon walked together, talking about the men who'd died, eating pear in narrow slivers that one of the housekeepers had cut up. They came to a shed of cages, breeding quarters for the serpents. There were shadows looping in the dark. Eyes peeping among the dried foliage. Haemon put his face against the glass of a tank and saw the spotted python holding a mouse carcass in its throat, and the slick blond-brownish twists of its body, and a spook of a mouth hinged with teeth like a picket fence along its jaw.

This was the snake Eteokles had loved the most. He'd had it since he was a boy. It was more than a metre long. In that gloomy tank the snake, which was named Sylvester Stallone, made barely any movement, using all its energy to consume the mice it was fed or drag its intestines through the gravel. Walking away from the shed, Haemon asked Antigone did she have a problem feeding the snakes? knowing the mice had been bred solely for the purposes of being killed and eaten. He knew she had a soft spot for living creatures. Antigone spoke sharply, 'Listen, you're hardly the RSPCA.'

Going out of the shed, the dogs padding along beside them seemed to swell and grow tense as they stepped back into the sunlight. The brightness, the balmy air, gave them an extraordinary summer-afternoon weightiness. Those snakes lying in silence in the shed behind, and Antigone and Haemon shuffling through the green flat grass toward the house where, from a slit window over the basement they heard something like the hiss of a radio tuned to one side of the band, and the small cobbled clang of Oedipus banging metal objects on the rust iron pipes that zigzagged across the walls and ceiling in his subterranean room.

active duty

    Underneath the King Street office was a café.
Square formica tables, red vinyl seats. Creon, his right-hand man,
and Tiresias and Haemon, having identified the bodies, sat
drinking coffee,
sat together trying to decide
    about the funerals, how to proceed.

    For hours.

    Creon, like Jocasta, thinks there should be a service for Eteokles
and nothing for his brother.
    Creon has control,
but there is the problem of Antigone.

    He takes off his glasses and pinches the bridge of nose
with two fingers.
The knuckles are bulbous and the nails are chewed to stubs.

    Haemon picks up his phone and goes to the corner,
taps out the number for Palis. The others frown and listen.

    In this light the scene approaches a dream. Except nothing
irreversibly bad happens in a dream,
nothing someone wouldn't be able to restore.

a brother's a brother

So Antigone explained to Haemon on the phone.
At Palis, half undressed on her bed, in her room, an immense,
light-filled loft with a chandelier and gold painted mouldings
on the ceiling.
She wore a long Nike singlet and vintage shell earings.
Brown hair, tawny brown, in knotty half-dreads.

This was the wired, all-buttons-pressed, strung-out Antigone
in her *Looking Glass* refuge, who had her friends on alert,
while her analyst, resuming the accustomed routine of appeasing
 wrote solicitous emails
at regular intervals to her from his office. Therapists, it seems,
 deal with their patients each in their own manner.

Antigone kept her go-fuck-yourself expression on her face.

Haemon on the other end of the line,
the others listening to him anxiously,
 asking, 'So, what's she saying now?'

The whole business of dealing with a difficult personality,
which seemed insurmountable,
 grief, which seemed insurmountable, her semi-pitying,

worried sister, Ismene, on the landing outside
raising both her arms above her head, thrumming on the door,

hoping some note of reason issuing from Haemon or the shrink
 would break the circuit, appeal
 to a taste for some emotional control
and the virtues of cooperation, and in the process calm things down.

Antigone's head was lifted, defiant, her mouth, tiny cracks with blood,
blood weeping in each corner. On the shadowed bed, sitting
hugging her knees, chandelier shards flashing like tin
in the shafts thrown through the windows catching the sunlight;

outside currawongs, glass-eyed and bolshy in the she-oaks,
    ebony beetles scuttling past beetles,
meat ants like the phalanxes of an empire.
    Under her analyst's orders

    and under that, the imagining of herself being dead,

    and emptiness.

The emptiness of Cook's creek in summer.

    The sensation of depletion, dizzying, brought on by nerves too often in flight.

She said to herself, there was a special kind of infinity,
    endlessness, that is produced when consumed by absence,
a hole of negativity so vast it becomes a positive space,
    spreading;
it expanded in her body, like smoke unrolling across a bushfire sky.

    She thought of Polyneices, her love for him, recalled

    the sight of him walking through the yard in the mornings,
those times at Cronulla she wished she'd agreed to go swimming with him,
    shooshing him, pulling her hat down over her head,
then lying on her towel in the shade till she'd gone to sleep.

These moments in their lives breathed a jealousy

that fractured her memory of everything. If she thought
about the losses, suffering,
there wasn't an image that didn't bring with it pain.

It was this Haemon didn't understand.

ismene speaks

    You see, like a river
has the fluid push
    to out-manoeuvre stone

    she steers swishing headwaters
against the banks,
    remarkable in their resistance,
my practised sister,

    the fiercest heart
I know of
    in the world.

parrhesia

    Antigone moves towards the door, cheeks
damp with sweat, puts the phone on speaker,
feels for her cigarettes on her desk – celebrity print-outs,
    local, not local, brassy as horns smiling up her –

she runs her tongue over her teeth, wets her lips,
    and asks if they're all listening
so the words will penetrate the group framing itself in opposition to her,

she's telling them – the metallic light
    softly disappearing, slipping down the wall –

    that truth,
and the freedom to speak that truth is all that matters,
    and, opening the door violently

    hurls herself downstairs with such force
it speaks a body's expectation of heaven.

tiresias on antigone

Creon strode out of the café with his voice blustering, but Tiresias would again say –

'She wants to play every part on her stage in order to find the part that is truly her.'

Desire corresponds to the condition of water.

basement blues

    Huddling in the bowely dark, under
the straggle of copper pipes that screw and ding over this space
    two-thirds griddle for decay,

    'Jocasta?' Oedipus, lovelorn,
drawn by the invisible heaving,
    weeping
till worn with dead-eye blinking,
calling across the shivering dark,
    'My sons? Daughters? Jocasta?'

speaking again

Ismene: Of what is gone, forever gone, all you can wish to reclaim is what is remembered, thoughts without rancour crusted on them, capable of picking you up off the floor and safekeeping your sanity when you feel you've nothing to go on with. Thoughts consoling and intimate. Work your will in ways that won't tempt the gods, or risk some spectacular calamity.

a message arrives

Late that afternoon, an email.

X-factor.

First round auditions.

White sun in big circles that are coming off the wall like thrown sequins.

'It's what we've waited for and you say, "It's not right. The light in enclosed spaces violates me."'

Pleading for reason, Jocasta, her hands held out to Antigone.

Ismene with a cat in her arms is watching from across the room. 'Listen, I will stand by you.'

Jocasta, 'Hear this, Antigone. You want to grow up.
While you've been carrying on Ismene
has had to shoulder the troubles of everyone here.
She loves you. She loved her brothers. And yet she knows
childish longings cannot mend wrongs,
that the dishonourable acts of black-hearted conspirators
cannot be altered with good words.

I said prayers, asked Polyneices to wait,
went down on my knees to Eteokles,
"Please…talk through things carefully…consider what we have…"

These are awkward times for all of us. Do as your sister does before even more is lost.'

The sentences pivoting around them,
wheeling and encircling Antigone,

and her sister throwing looks like vines at her.

And then there is there, in the background,
the silhouette of a god,

or monster,

contemplating the scene.

oedipus, the impetus

    And this is how he sees her,
singing songs, there in the living room,
his sad and vulnerable girl,
his daughter,
a musician who fears performing
a child of gen X,
a woman who falls in love easily,
a student of geometry,
and herself,
a mystic with a cynic's heart,
a fighter,
her dreams an agony,
her cries extinguished in
her peaceless head, chest, hips,
her foal-like body, with its seemingly
endless ambivalences
on what it wants to keep
and what it wants to leave behind,
someone who is full of oaths
and melodious whispers,
who sometimes sweats when the wind is biting
and who doles out promises
    to show a loyalty
without giving a second thought,
turns obsessed with feverish insistence,
and loses herself,
    senses nothing
but a melancholy night,
addresses the ghosts
that are flocking the house, migrating,

to where they hope to
escape the violence
in the air of Oyster Bay and dance
with her in the shadows.

creon's routine

Screwing coloured cables into white wall mountings with deadly speed.

where the nervous system never lets up

From the inarticulate sounds that come and go all day over his head Oedipus' heart congeals inside him.

What can all the pandemonium mean?

'God get me out of here!'

breakout

    Yes, he's in whipped up state, a near-delirium. Everyone's distracted
and peril can be swung round the room like a chair: dried sweat
on his neck, his stomach, streaked rivulets on his back:
wife, daughters, in-laws, the whole lot
    caught up in the drama.

    Yes, they see the disgraced old man step
across the Persian rug in front of the fireplace
to feel the lip of the piano, the edge of the piano keys,
and pitch a world, strained
to its perimeters, like a boat blowing off the Heads.
They see a pair of rapidly moving hands
skim and play with trembling force and hammer onto
the smooth tongues of the keyboard:
he throws his whole self into it, as if into a mountain lake –
and nothing falls so direct as that body's weight
into the water's dispersing currents;
he sinks like a branch snapped, its length
half submerged in places.

They see an array of ornaments abruptly
tilt and rock with a trembling quake
and sway into a dupe of aliveness,
wave and reel and roll the air as though readying
    to embrace them
or as if to raise their painted arms
and push the lot of them from a great distance
backwards on the floor. The cast figures
see-sawed there on the mantle
like an ensemble of dancing girls before a camera,
attempting to hold position. Courting couples,

clowns and swans, all immortalised in ceramic,
unnoticed as he plays across the room –
notes that crash like a branch snapped,
half-submerged in places.

    And then they see the figures' brown-gold forms
tumble onto the slate tiles of the fireplace in a mad
shattering of glass, porcelain, china, see him
    jolt, Oedipus,
stunned: and a strange feeling comes over them.

    They put the pieces together in pile, slouch away, stepping
over broken things, scared and sadder and sadder…

There he goes towards the doorway now,
but he lets them pass. He watches
and soon he's just standing there in his red shirt and soft brown suit,
    looking down the empty hall.
There's rain outside the window and
it streams all down the glass… A sound in his chest
like a branch snapped, half submerged in places.

    Oh, but Antigone…

    Swift – she races upstairs.
She rushes from the atrium to her room, makes herself
into the goddess element. Everyone here
within Palis's walls withdraws whenever this happens,
relying on habit with resigned shrugs; it's a way to do things
if it's what you're used to.

    'Is it right? Is it fair?'

She stands shouting down through the balustrades.

    She gets more difficult, throws herself to the floor and counts to ten before an answer reaches her –

    Ismene pleaded in weary labour
through the gold and warm, shaft and white lines, strip and glow,
appealing with cries and gentle rawness – so that
Antigone heard with feeling more than ears –
grief in her bones, grief with her mind, and understanding
her home as a battle field, she thought,

    Someone take the curse off this family!

while hot-pulsed tensions were so implacable
    that the staff hid,
shut themselves in a deep long-communal
muteness, which for reasons of discretion and job safety
    were of good use, naturally.

    And then, Jocasta on the roof, the household
not saying anything, not asking, not not asking,
the grey line of the matriarch's cheekbones drawn,
her dress flickering in the hazy gusts,
her far-off gaze the furthest-off gaze, the gaze that says,
Let me leave now, it is all too late,
as she falls forward over the ledge into the white window of air.

    Cameras on the eaves. Inside the control room
Creon's men saw her plunging there, front and centre,
and radioed Creon, who just pulled out his phone
and called the relevant authorities.

    Haemon, having followed his father, told Antigone
this story, parts of which she accepted and
parts of which she didn't accept at all:

   'She walks out onto the rooftop like a Buddha, your mother, eyes slow,
black eyes looking out, looking at nobody. One of the controllers
calls us over, points to one of the screens. There's leaves
and feathers all over and she steps across, raises her face to the sky
and moves her head from side to side like she's cooling herself
in a breeze. We watch from the room downstairs and soon she's just
    standing there
between two parapets, dangling her arms
like she's posing or something. Fading light now,
not light not dark. Sun washes over her body as if she's transparent and she's
just standing up there on that roof, demented. She shouldn't be there:
my father sends up a man. This is about eight o'clock and he's waiting to leave
for the track, pushing down on the buttons to put the lights
on because if under a spot she'll maybe stop.

   I see her step closer to the gutter where the corner is
and she hears the door open and turns and sees the guy.
At first he tries to come close, but she reaches out
her arms to say no and she begins shaking.
His body starts shaking too. He's on his own with her,
but trusts it won't be for long. There's three of them making
their way up now, because they can tell what it is that's on her mind.
And I'm thinking all of a sudden about all the men-eyes she's had
glinting through gooey slits at her
and how she's wrecked things. And I'm sort of furious
because I know she's had the right idea a lot of times

counselling family as well as business, though
of course on a different scale, but too much of what she's said
doesn't work in real life. At the same time I felt, well,
I felt like kind of hypnotised.

    (Why am I hesitating to tell you this?
I don't want you to think I didn't want to help her.)

    Yes, when she tipped over
the edge, my father tossed his form guide
into the bin, grabbing his phone from the desk
and straight away called an ambulance.
You know, when they take her off I see all the dogs try
to follow the scent of her.
There is a horrible sadness issuing from this broken family.
    What hope is left?
Misunderstanding has deranged the lot of you, dear
crazy Antigone.
You're sweet and talented,
but your love, too, is lopsided.

    Retreat, please. You say you're sick of all those contests
for everything, but why do you still fight?
To be in the grip of all this suffering and all this
grief… Perhaps you do like it after all.
But me, I hate this balancing act.
My father hanging on to his ideas for the two of us,
you love-worn if nothing else.
My father hanging on
because he thinks we're young enough
to get over things and be together.

But I don't know, I'm not so sure. And what to do,
what to do about your father...

    You say love isn't divined
by honour so I suppose that's
what makes you insist on the way in which Polyneices
is put to rest. But there's not a chance Creon
will hear of it. Your brother
brought his entourage here, deployed his men
because he wanted to destroy
    his own family's empire.
So much else now needs to be seen to.

    Enough, whatever else now, enough.
I know my father is serious when he says
we will bury Jocasta with her son,
    Eteokles:
Polyneices will be disposed of in other parts.'

waiting

    In the hall there is rain filling the window

    and the window and the window
and there is Oedipus
    trying to hear what's going on outside.

    'She is gone. She is not with us. She will not be back.'

Then silence.

And silence.

A sound of nothing that stays with him all his life.

edict

    Palis.

The hall.

Its door.

Ragged light on rose marble.

'Leave this city Oedipus. Your time is done.
    You must never return, pitiful man.'

Turning briskly, Creon puts his hand under the old bloke's jaw,
    tightens his fingers round his neck,

Then Creon, 'Out!' Shoves him with such force
Oedipus' head crashes against the jamb.

When they got round to the question of what to do
    with Antigone
Creon tries to make her concentrate
    on being with his son.

She says, 'You won't let me bury my brother?
Well, fuck you! I'll kill your son so you'll know what I feel!'
How good it is, she thinks, to proclaim independence.

So Creon rolls the flesh back from his eyes, says to her
    'Go! Be out by morning.
And take your father,
and your dogs and serpents. Go
the lot of you, or I swear
    you will die.'

family

    Antigone spends her last few hours in Palis with Ismene. Her sister with her head on Antigone's breast,

    'When we were small we dreamed like musicians.'

Ismene and Antigone had their first happinesses while singing. The marvel of poetry. The marvel of sound rising obliquely
    like moth wings flying.

    'What is life compared to that?'
'What is anything compared to anything?'

liberty

'Your last sighs, father,' said Antigone, 'in the measure
of the world that was once inhabited by my mother,
   my brothers.

Hurry, pack now. This morning the house is rimmed
in red sun, the windows over-lit
   as though with blood.
I can hardly breathe, the air is so thick with it.

   To think of what has happened in a single day!

   Now we must grope toward another place,
not happy with our lives, but in the care of each other.

   So here, take this stick to help guide you. We will walk
through the yellow grass and purple hydrangeas,
make our way across the country as travellers coming
from a dark cavern into the warm afternoon.'

sea change

    Bobbing under a sliver of moon. Sydney sunrise.
A row-boat, kelpfishes jumping,
tea-tree and cragged heads of banksia on the shore.
Something moving in the greenery, a small creature scrabbles away.
One of the dogs pricks up his ears. Up the ridge
the stilted houses cling to the scrub. Windows flash.
The two exiles wrinkle the air. Gripping the oars with all her strength,
Antigone pulls them slowly through the film and keeping
a rhythm steers them to their schooner.
She listens to the slap slap. They duck a gull.

Here is the one thing they have left to them. Oedipus' yacht.
A small cabin they can sleep in, bed under the bow, windows,
table, shower, and here's the camp-stove.
While they're sailing north, this is where they'll cut and cook things.
Settling her father below deck, Antigone
goes out, checks the halyards and raises the sails.
She clamps the ropes and calls down to her father,
lets him know they're off. Then she angles for the Heads, and they're at sea,
all sea around them: the water's an overdone colour that grazes
and cracks and cracks between the invisible and the curved sky.

For eight days they sail like that.
Antigone can see their skin is red now. They sleep in turns.
The dried gobs of salt sticking the pillow to their necks.
Three days the wind was a white filth, all fists. The clouds
sat heavy and glowered while the sails smacked.
When he was above board, Oedipus clung to the side
like a mallee root. Antigone wrapped a long thin arm around his shoulder
and pressed her cheek down into the groove of his collarbone and curled
his hair behind his ear. Round the dog-eared rim her cold fingers

fixed strings of dreadlock and brushing past sideburns like wool,
neck glanced by her mouth, down went cobwebs of tears over his scapula
through flutes of ribs and into soft grey and copper mattings cloaking
his belly, his body rocking with waves, soft warm sobs, he
stroked her head, her hair flicking
flicking sharp as tussock across his chin and nose,
his chest and shanks pelted by wails and ocean wet and widened.
And then the sea brought up a sun that tapered through the nebula,
striking the world's lid, and there they were, far flung still from land,
but they could tell they were getting closer.
Then they set their rods off the back
and lift from underneath them a big perch that lasts for two days.

For them life is simplified; sleep, eat, sail. On the tenth day
the northern hills come into sight, a roll of duney forest and ironbark
and ironbark and pure sky. They step onto the daisy-white sand,
two figures, one, cold and slight as a peg, one like exposed bone,
two rangy dogs. Crossing the beach and up and up and up.
In the mountains Antigone's head is full of bleak thoughts. Lying
in the shack of one her father's few loyal old associates, she has her arms
covering her eyes so that she cannot see what her father doesn't see.
His voice moaning, 'Ah, I'm a man who once had it all, now
banished… Yes, though
I know there were mistakes made along the way –'
She stops him. 'No more. I've left friends too. My sister. Friends…'

    Yes, this is it,
they can do nothing but what's needed to survive,
Oedipus sitting like a crackpot on the slope,
muttering muttering *homeless, homeless*, until night
comes on, always his head somewhere else,
veins in his neck swelling and sweat sliding
down his arms, glad of the tentative voices

the trees make dimly over the surf; Antigone,
setting scraps of food on the makeshift table, her hopes thin
as dust, though there are the images, alive and recurrent,
thousands of over-lit memories to which she's attached,
and melodies, words,
that merge with difficult emotion,
and appear in the margins of her postcards to her analyst…

'This is a new world.
And I am writing songs. And
the songs are alive. Finally,
I am an artist…'

The hours disappear over the hills and ocean.
As she's slicing some sort of apple, her insistently roaming mind
thinks again on music, and on death, the simple matter of it;
    death of a mother, death of a brother and a brother,

the difference death makes to the heart in you.

www.ingramcontent.com/pod-product-compliance
Lightning Source LLC
Chambersburg PA
CBHW062154100526
44589CB00014B/1838